Editor
Mary S. Jones

Managing Editor
Karen J. Goldfluss, M.S. Ed.

Cover Artist
Barb Lorseyedi

Art Production Manager
Kevin Barnes

Imaging
Craig Gunnell

Publisher
Mary D. Smith, M.S. Ed.

Practice Makes Perfect Number Puzzles
GRADE 3

Author
Mary Rosenberg

Teacher Created Resources, Inc.
6421 Industry Way
Westminster, CA 92683
www.teachercreated.com

ISBN-1-4206-3908-0

©*2006 Teacher Created Resources, Inc.*

Made in U.S.A.

The classroom teacher may reproduce copies of materials in this book for classroom use only. The reproduction of any part for an entire school or school system is strictly prohibited. No part of this publication may be transmitted, stored, or recorded in any form without written permission from the publisher.

Table of Contents

Introduction 3
Puzzle 1: Thousands of Numbers 4
Puzzle 2: What's the Number? 5
Puzzle 3: Numbers in the Thousands 6
Puzzle 4: Numbers in the Ten Thousands 7
Puzzle 5: Value of a Digit 8
Puzzle 6: Comparing Numbers 9
Puzzle 7: Which Number Is Larger? 10
Puzzle 8: Rounding On! 11
Puzzle 9: Numbers by the Thousands 12
Puzzle 10: Numbers in the Ten Thousands 13
Puzzle 11: Subtraction Fun 14
Puzzle 12: Subtraction in the Ten Thousands 15
Puzzle 13: Adding and Subtracting Practice 16
Puzzle 14: Mixed Practice: Adding and Subtracting 17
Puzzle 15: Ten Thousand Numbers 18
Puzzle 16: 5, 4, 3, 2, 1, Multiply! 19
Puzzle 17: Warming Up to Multiplication 20
Puzzle 18: Multiplication Fun 21
Puzzle 19: Name That Factor! 22
Puzzle 20: Easy to Divide 23
Puzzle 21: More Division Practice 24
Puzzle 22: Mixed Practice: Multiplication and Division 25
Puzzle 23: Deciphering Decimals 26
Puzzle 24: Adding Decimals 27
Puzzle 25: Subtracting Decimals 28
Puzzle 26: Adding and Subtracting Decimals 29
Puzzle 27: Money, Money, Money 30
Puzzle 28: More Money, Money, Money 31
Puzzle 29: Does Anybody Have the Time? 32
Puzzle 30: Minute by Minute 33–34
Puzzle 31: Pockets Full of Money 35–36
Puzzle 32: At the Game Shop 37–38
Puzzle 33: Party Supplies 39–40
Puzzle 34: Arts and Crafts Store 41–42
Answer Key 43–48

Introduction

The old adage "practice makes perfect" can really hold true for your child and his or her education. The more practice and exposure your child has with concepts being taught in school, the more success he or she is likely to find. For many parents, knowing how to help your children can be frustrating because the resources may not be readily available. As a parent it is also difficult to know where to focus your efforts so that the extra practice your child receives at home supports what he or she is learning in school.

This book has been designed to help both parents and teachers reinforce basic math skills. *Practice Makes Perfect* reviews basic math skills for children in grade 3. This book contains number puzzles that allow children to learn, review, and reinforce basic math concepts. While it would be impossible to include all concepts taught in grade 3 in this book, the following main objectives are reinforced through practice exercises:

- addition
- comparing numbers
- division
- money
- multiplication

- naming shapes
- place value
- rounding
- standard form
- subtraction

There are 34 puzzles organized sequentially, so children can build their knowledge from more basic skills to higher-level math skills. Number puzzles are designed for students to review math concepts and have fun practicing them.

How to Make the Most of This Book

Here are some useful ideas for optimizing the practice pages in this book:

- Set aside a specific place in your home to work on the practice pages. Keep it neat and tidy with materials on hand.

- Set up a certain time of day to work on the puzzles. This will establish consistency. An alternative is to look for times in your day or week that are less hectic and conducive to practicing skills.

- Keep all practice sessions with your child positive and constructive. If the mood becomes tense, or you and your child are frustrated, set the book aside and look for another time to practice with your child.

- Help with instructions if necessary. If your child is having difficulty understanding what to do or how to get started, work through the first problem with him or her.

- Review the work your child has done. This serves as reinforcement and provides further practice.

- Pay attention to the areas in which your child has the most difficulty. Provide extra guidance and exercises in those areas. Allowing children to use drawings and manipulatives, such as coins, tiles, or flash cards, can help them grasp difficult concepts more easily.

- Look for ways to make real-life applications to the skills being reinforced.

Standard Form

Puzzle 1

Thousands of Numbers

Write each number in standard form and complete the number puzzle.

Across

2. Seven thousand, four hundred eighty-six _____
4. Four thousand, four hundred fifty-two _____
5. Nine thousand, one hundred seventy-six _____
6. Nine thousand, nine hundred thirty-six _____
8. Three thousand, eight hundred twenty-one _____
11. Eight thousand, two hundred fifty-three _____
12. Nine thousand, six hundred fifty _____
13. Seven thousand, three hundred sixty-three _____
15. Seven thousand, two hundred seventy _____
18. Seven thousand, six hundred sixty-nine _____
19. One thousand, one hundred forty-two _____

Down

1. Six thousand, five hundred thirty-seven _____
3. Eight thousand, eight hundred twenty-nine _____
7. Eight thousand, nine _____
9. One thousand, two hundred fifty-six _____
10. Five thousand, seven _____
11. Eight thousand, four hundred thirty-seven _____
14. Three thousand, one hundred eighty-six _____
16. Two thousand, eight hundred fourteen _____
17. Five thousand, two hundred thirty-three _____

4 #3908 Practice Makes Perfect: Number Puzzles © Teacher Created Resources, Inc.

Standard Form

Puzzle 2

What's the Number?

Write each number in standard form and complete the number puzzle.

Across

2. Seventy-eight thousand, seven hundred ten _____
3. Sixty-four thousand, one hundred two _____
4. Fifty-nine thousand, nine hundred thirty-six _____
7. Ninety-four thousand, three hundred twenty-four _____
11. Seventy-four thousand, eight hundred seventy-two _____
12. Seventy thousand, two hundred sixty-one _____
14. Fifty thousand, two hundred eighty-eight _____
15. Fifty-three thousand, three hundred eighty _____
16. Thirty-nine thousand, one hundred sixty-four _____
17. Fifty-four thousand, six hundred eighty-eight _____

Down

1. Twenty-four thousand, seven hundred fifty-six _____
2. Seventy-four thousand, two hundred eighty-nine _____
5. Sixty-nine thousand, four hundred twenty _____
6. Fifty-two thousand, one hundred two _____
8. Sixty-seven thousand, nine hundred ninety-three _____
9. Fifty-eight thousand, one hundred thirty-eight _____
10. Forty-one thousand, eight hundred fifty-eight _____
13. Sixty-seven thousand, two hundred thirty-nine _____
15. Fifty-one thousand, seven hundred fifty-two _____
16. Thirty-one thousand, six hundred six _____

Standard Form

Puzzle 3

Numbers in the Thousands

Write each sum in standard form and complete the number puzzle.

Across

3. 9,000 + 500 + 10 + 5 = _____
6. 9,000 + 20 = _____
7. 7,000 + 600 + 30 + 2 = _____
10. 3,000 + 700 + 4 = _____
12. 4,000 + 200 + 40 + 6 = _____
13. 8,000 + 100 + 60 + 8 = _____
15. 1,000 + 80 + 1 = _____
16. 5,000 + 100 + 80 + 7 = _____
18. 5,000 + 400 + 90 = _____

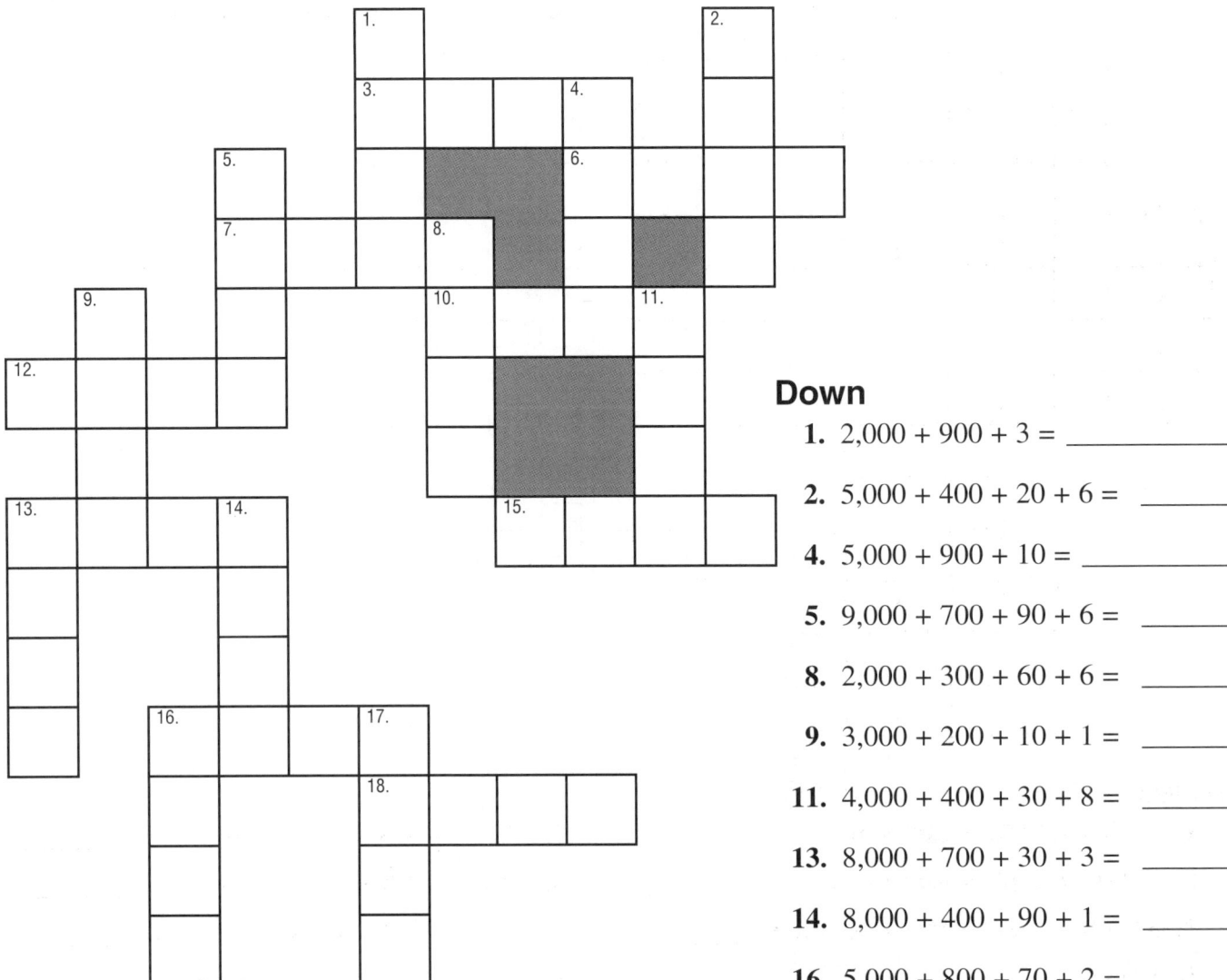

Down

1. 2,000 + 900 + 3 = _____
2. 5,000 + 400 + 20 + 6 = _____
4. 5,000 + 900 + 10 = _____
5. 9,000 + 700 + 90 + 6 = _____
8. 2,000 + 300 + 60 + 6 = _____
9. 3,000 + 200 + 10 + 1 = _____
11. 4,000 + 400 + 30 + 8 = _____
13. 8,000 + 700 + 30 + 3 = _____
14. 8,000 + 400 + 90 + 1 = _____
16. 5,000 + 800 + 70 + 2 = _____
17. 7,000 + 500 + 90 + 7 = _____

Standard Form

Puzzle 4
Numbers in the Ten Thousands

Write each sum in standard form and complete the number puzzle.

Across

2. 30,000 + 8,000 + 700 + 20 + 4 = _____
4. 70,000 + 7,000 + 900 + 30 + 6 = _____
9. 80,000 + 2,000 + 300 + 30 + 5 = _____
10. 80,000 + 3,000 + 800 + 1 = _____
11. 50,000 + 7,000 + 800 + 5 = _____
12. 20,000 + 4,000 + 900 + 20 + 2 = _____
14. 20,000 + 9,000 + 900 + 90 + 6 = _____
16. 40,000 + 8,000 + 100 + 10 + 5 = _____
18. 40,000 + 4,000 + 800 + 7 = _____
19. 50,000 + 1,000 + 2 = _____
20. 70,000 + 1,000 + 600 + 90 + 6 = _____

Down

1. 70,000 + 5,000 + 300 + 40 + 9 = _____
2. 30,000 + 9,000 + 600 + 8 = _____
3. 60,000 + 7,000 + 800 + 30 + 8 = _____
5. 50,000 + 2,000 + 100 + 60 + 9 = _____
6. 10,000 + 100 + 50 + 2 = _____
7. 30,000 + 8,000 + 200 + 80 + 2 = _____
8. 70,000 + 4,000 + 60 + 3 = _____
13. 20,000 + 2,000 + 800 + 30 + 8 = _____
15. 60,000 + 4,000 + 400 + 60 + 1 = _____
17. 10,000 + 2,000 + 300 + 60 + 9 = _____

Place Value

Puzzle 5
Value of a Digit

Read each clue. Write the number from the Number Bank that matches the clue in the number puzzle.

Across
2. 6 in the thousands place
3. 8 in the thousands place
5. 0 in the ones place
6. 1 in the ten thousands place
8. the largest number that has a 2 in the thousands place
9. 9 in the ones place
10. 6 in the ones place
11. 1 in the tens place
14. 0 in the thousands place
15. the smaller number that has a 3 in the thousands place
16. 7 in the ten thousands place

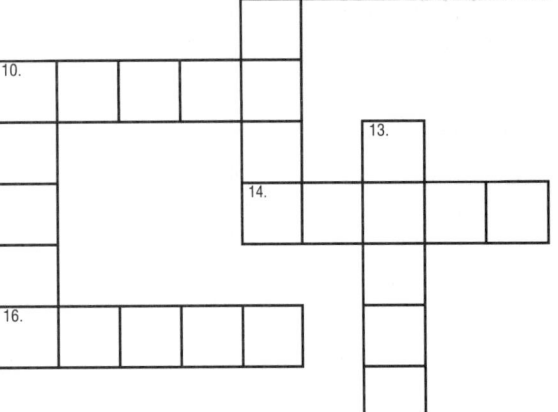

Down
1. 5 in the thousands place
2. the smaller number that has a 7 in the ones place
3. 8 in the hundreds place
4. 2 in the ones place
7. 5 in the hundreds place
8. the largest number that has a 9 in the ten thousands place
10. 4 in the thousands place
12. the largest number that has a 3 in the ones place
13. 3 in the ten thousands place

Number Bank

17,498	58,671	77,688
29,282	59,480	80,901
39,393	61,159	83,425
42,613	62,746	92,921
51,187	64,367	93,591
56,135	65,083	97,648
57,834	67,143	

Puzzle 6

Comparing Numbers

Use the symbols > (greater than) or < (less than) to compare each set of numbers. Write the **smaller** number in the number puzzle.

Across

3. 6,396 _____ 5,789
4. 8,449 _____ 5,545
7. 6,254 _____ 1,754
9. 9,117 _____ 2,779
11. 9,581 _____ 6,357
12. 2,183 _____ 3,691
14. 7,013 _____ 7,255
16. 2,043 _____ 9,402

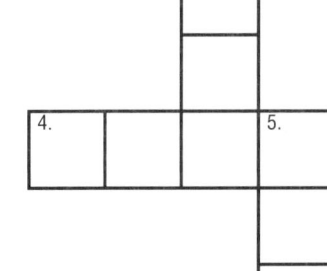
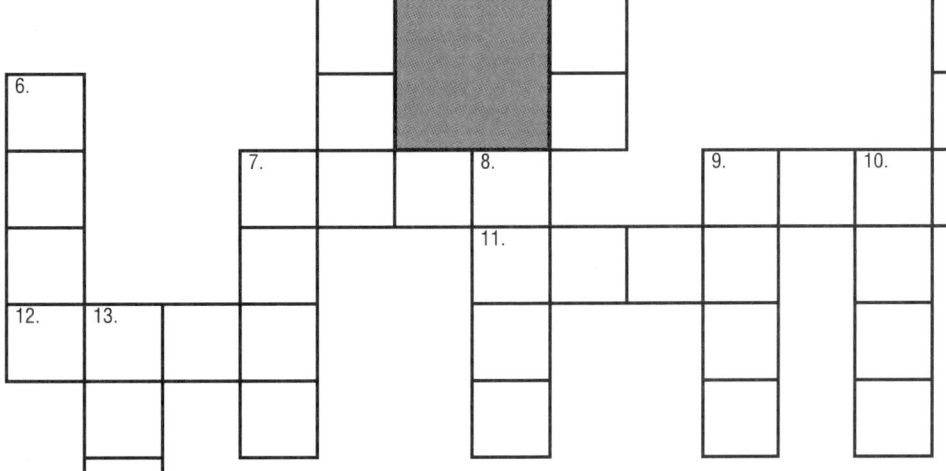
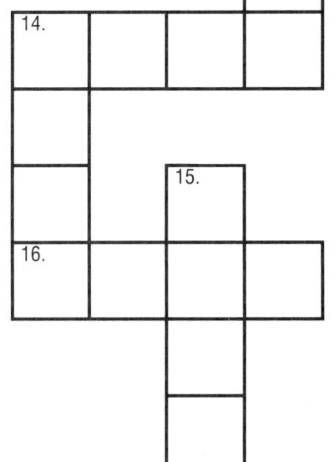

Down

1. 8,803 _____ 3,024
2. 9,514 _____ 6,948
3. 5,717 _____ 9,084
5. 6,685 _____ 5,259
6. 3,062 _____ 3,460
7. 5,010 _____ 1,432
8. 8,952 _____ 4,650
9. 8,639 _____ 2,791
10. 7,463 _____ 8,852
13. 1,063 _____ 5,697
14. 8,782 _____ 7,912
15. 9,313 _____ 8,444

Comparing Numbers

Puzzle 7

Which Number Is Larger?

Use the symbols > (greater than) or < (less than) to compare each set of numbers. Write the **larger** number in the number puzzle.

Across
1. 615 _____ 352
2. 510 _____ 953
3. 740 _____ 300
5. 110 _____ 922
6. 839 _____ 984
8. 567 _____ 347
12. 424 _____ 678
13. 504 _____ 519
14. 960 _____ 512
15. 887 _____ 602

Down
1. 523 _____ 637
2. 912 _____ 721
4. 165 _____ 489
5. 965 _____ 753
7. 826 _____ 298
9. 649 _____ 503
10. 580 _____ 118
11. 750 _____ 413
14. 937 _____ 664

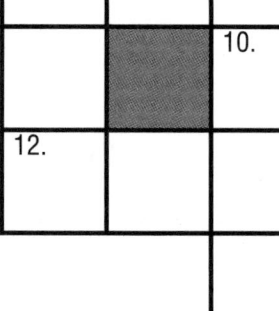

6 is larger than 2!

Puzzle 8

Rounding On!

Round each number to the nearest ten, hundred, or thousand. Complete the number puzzle.

Across

1. Round 89 to the nearest ten. _____
2. Round 11 to the nearest ten. _____
3. Round 27 to the nearest ten. _____
5. Round 443 to the nearest hundred. _____
7. Round 31 to the nearest ten. _____
9. Round 7,182 to the nearest thousand. _____
10. Round 9,575 to the nearest thousand. _____
11. Round 545 to the nearest hundred. _____
12. Round 699 to the nearest hundred. _____
13. Round 5,057 to the nearest thousand. _____
14. Round 221 to the nearest hundred. _____

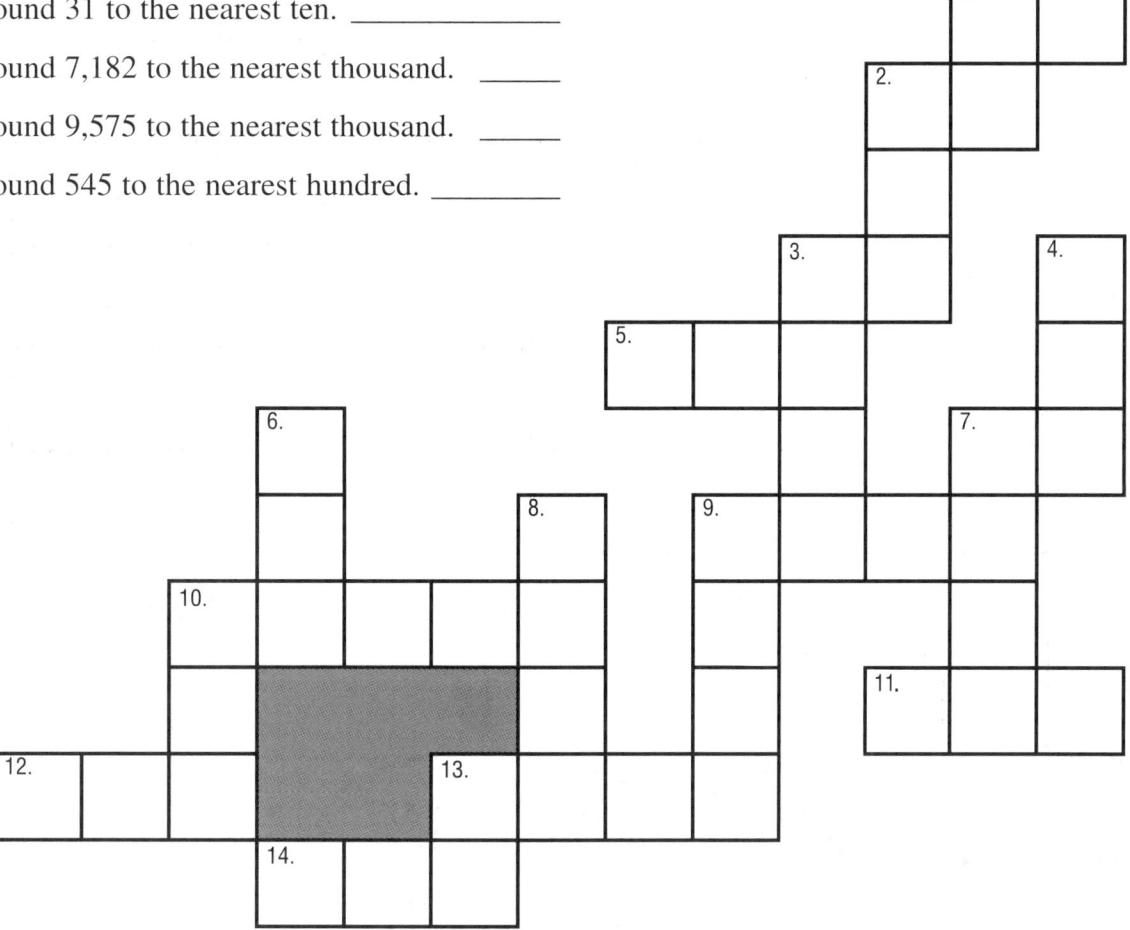

Down

1. Round 94 to the nearest ten. _____
2. Round 96 to the nearest hundred. _____
3. Round 2,631 to the nearest thousand. _____
4. Round 377 to the nearest hundred. _____
6. Round 762 to the nearest hundred. _____
7. Round 3,388 to the nearest thousand. _____
8. Round 8,507 to the nearest thousand. _____
9. Round 6,514 to the nearest thousand. _____
10. Round 131 to the nearest hundred. _____
13. Round 46 to the nearest ten. _____

Addition (Thousands)

Puzzle 9

Numbers by the Thousands

Solve each addition problem. Write each sum in the number puzzle.

Across

3. 279 + 1,858 = _____
5. 3,754 + 802 = _____
6. 364 + 5,102 = _____
10. 475 + 6,673 = _____
12. 6,744 + 1,977 = _____
13. 2,432 + 7,122 = _____
15. 6,709 + 2,309 = _____
18. 1,342 + 3,216 = _____
19. 5,829 + 1,885 = _____

Down

1. 5,067 + 149 = _____
2. 8,416 + 829 = _____
4. 165 + 3,490 = _____
7. 902 + 3,532 = _____
8. 591 + 4,480 = _____
9. 6,885 + 3,010 = _____
11. 6,739 + 1,559 = _____
14. 3,276 + 972 = _____
15. 1,844 + 7,953 = _____
16. 5,650 + 3,876 = _____
17. 1,814 + 3,669 = _____

Addition (Ten Thousands)

Puzzle 10

Numbers in the Ten Thousands

Solve each addition problem. Write each sum in the number puzzle.

Across
2. 57,899 + 32,007 = _____
5. 70,548 + 28,504 = _____
7. 48,960 + 50,767 = _____
8. 21,681 + 54,367 = _____
9. 4,347 + 39,928 = _____
10. 32,271 + 41,893 = _____
12. 1,492 + 84,907 = _____

16. 6,145 + 34,909 = _____
17. 64,690 + 17,391 = _____
18. 3,403 + 81,754 = _____
19. 4,329 + 87,781 = _____

Down
1. 7,052 + 48,609 = _____
3. 84,139 + 10,459 = _____
4. 83,116 + 13,228 = _____
5. 53,279 + 38,856 = _____
6. 43,672 + 16,112 = _____

11. 2,962 + 15,723 = _____
13. 6,145 + 92,730 = _____
14. 6,678 + 55,821 = _____
15. 8,641 + 35,930 = _____

Subtraction (Thousands)

Puzzle 11

Subtraction Fun

Solve each subtraction problem. Write each difference in the number puzzle.

Across

1. 7,854 − 792 = _____
4. 8,828 − 3,908 = _____
5. 7,975 − 312 = _____
7. 8,731 − 5,380 = _____
8. 8,494 − 125 = _____
10. 7,741 − 2,106 = _____
12. 9,611 − 5,304 = _____
13. 5,038 − 3,029 = _____
15. 3,990 − 142 = _____
16. 3,111 − 801 = _____
18. 9,472 − 540 = _____

Down

2. 7,565 − 922 = _____
3. 4,574 − 2,491 = _____
5. 7,976 − 442 = _____
6. 9,426 − 2,291 = _____
9. 9,888 − 361 = _____
11. 9,605 − 3,535 = _____
13. 2,805 − 623 = _____
14. 6,540 − 730 = _____
17. 6,541 − 3,207 = _____

Puzzle 12

Subtraction in the Ten Thousands

Solve each subtraction problem. Write each difference in the number puzzle.

Across

1. 62,409 – 1,194 = _____
6. 86,720 – 1,210 = _____
7. 47,180 – 7,073 = _____
9. 39,822 – 3,810 = _____
10. 34,711 – 4,550 = _____
12. 98,790 – 91,610 = _____
13. 93,878 – 58,851 = _____
14. 87,710 – 69,410 = _____
15. 48,007 – 29,005 = _____
17. 83,325 – 36,221 = _____

Down

1. 62,826 – 1,916 = _____
2. 53,459 – 2,916 = _____
3. 35,948 – 26,236 = _____
4. 90,116 – 1,006 = _____
5. 58,169 – 3,753 = _____
8. 80,754 – 5,654 = _____
10. 50,504 – 20,330 = _____
11. 69,041 – 23,330 = _____
13. 98,294 – 61,753 = _____
16. 68,340 – 40,900 = _____

Addition and Subtraction (Thousands)

Puzzle 13
Adding and Subtracting Practice

Solve each problem. Write each answer in the number puzzle.

Across

2. 8,697 − 1,206 = _____
5. 6,974 − 3,945 = _____
6. 6,129 + 2,580 = _____
9. 3,295 + 6,632 = _____
10. 8,359 − 8,075 = _____
11. 5,471 − 4,109 = _____
14. 2,024 + 3,278 = _____
16. 6,416 + 2,762 = _____
17. 8,511 − 8,300 = _____
19. 1,075 + 6,200 = _____

Down

1. 3,247 + 2,517 = _____
3. 8,410 − 7,230 = _____
4. 2,533 + 4,544 = _____
7. 2,399 + 5,350 = _____
8. 2,950 + 7,011 = _____
12. 6,688 − 2,830 = _____
13. 7,441 − 7,140 = _____
15. 9,812 − 9,521 = _____
18. 6,809 − 5,686 = _____

Addition and Subtraction (Thousands)

Puzzle 14

Mixed Practice: Adding and Subtracting

Solve each problem. Write each answer in the number puzzle.

Across

1. 6,854 – 4,391 = _____
3. 4,612 + 5,540 = _____
5. 8,371 – 7,426 = _____
7. 3,162 – 1,209 = _____
11. 3,283 + 4,943 = _____
13. 5,296 – 1,607 = _____
14. 5,343 – 3,762 = _____
16. 7,755 – 1,971 = _____
17. 5,972 + 7,317 = _____
18. 2,436 + 5,736 = _____

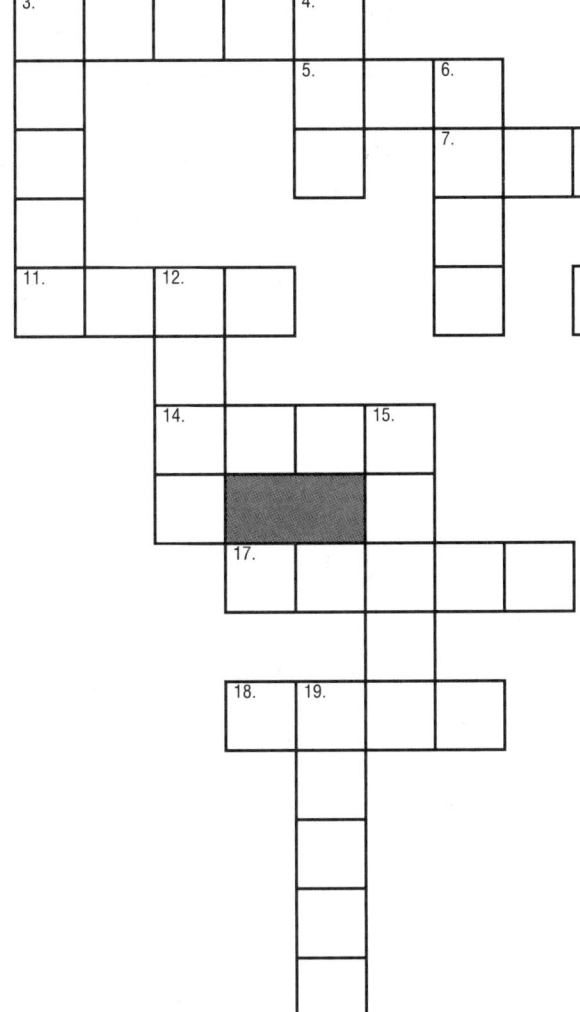

Down

2. 1,996 – 1,665 = _____
3. 4,826 + 6,572 = _____
4. 2,848 – 2,556 = _____
6. 6,175 – 1,020 = _____
8. 1,179 + 2,383 = _____
9. 1,046 + 4,881 = _____
10. 1,780 + 4,894 = _____
12. 1,090 + 1,529 = _____
15. 6,048 + 8,189 = _____
19. 7,572 + 8,829 = _____

Addition and Subtraction (Ten Thousands)

Puzzle 15

Ten Thousand Numbers

Solve each problem. Complete the number puzzle.

Across

1. 36,637 + 23,149 = _____
3. 18,352 + 51,229 = _____
5. 37,984 − 20,810 = _____
6. 73,311 − 65,210 = _____
8. 17,564 + 73,433 = _____
10. 21,268 + 39,430 = _____
11. 13,970 + 36,010 = _____
13. 92,536 − 61,445 = _____
15. 19,925 + 39,044 = _____
16. 46,452 − 24,137 = _____
17. 98,244 − 75,205 = _____

Down

2. 52,704 + 36,287 = _____
4. 15,658 + 72,521 = _____
5. 98,297 − 83,169 = _____
6. 25,322 + 61,727 = _____
7. 74,028 − 33,018 = _____
9. 58,765 − 27,864 = _____
12. 54,099 − 50,038 = _____
13. 25,329 + 14,632 = _____
14. 44,765 − 19,213 = _____

18   #3908 Practice Makes Perfect: Number Puzzles   © Teacher Created Resources, Inc.

Puzzle 16

5, 4, 3, 2, 1, Multiply!

Solve each multiplication problem. Write each product as a **number word** in the number puzzle. See #2 Across. It has been done for you.

Across

2. 2 x 2 = 4
3. 1 x 0 = ___
4. 4 x 4 = ___
8. 1 x 5 = ___
9. 5 x 2 = ___
10. 3 x 2 = ___
12. 1 x 2 = ___
13. 5 x 5 = ___
15. 4 x 2 = ___
17. 3 x 1 = ___
18. 1 x 1 = ___

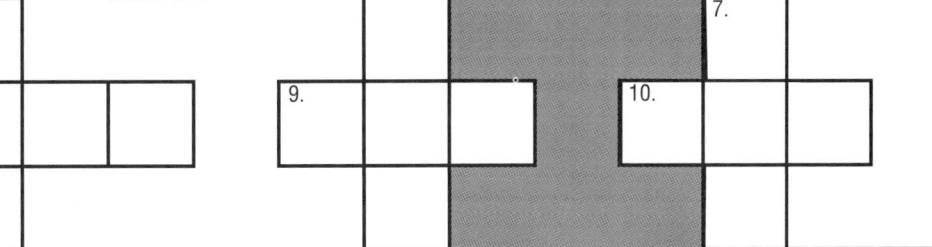

Down

1. 4 x 3 = ___
2. 2 x 2 = ___
5. 4 x 5 = ___
6. 2 x 4 = ___
7. 5 x 3 = ___
11. 5 x 1 = ___
14. 3 x 3 = ___
16. 2 x 5 = ___
17. 2 x 1 = ___

One-Digit Multipliers and Two-Digit Multiplicands

Puzzle 17

Warming Up to Multiplication

Solve each multiplication problem. Write each product in the number puzzle.

Across

4. 19 x 4 = _____
6. 67 x 2 = _____
8. 22 x 8 = _____
9. 73 x 5 = _____
11. 86 x 7 = _____
13. 79 x 6 = _____
15. 42 x 9 = _____
16. 98 x 6 = _____

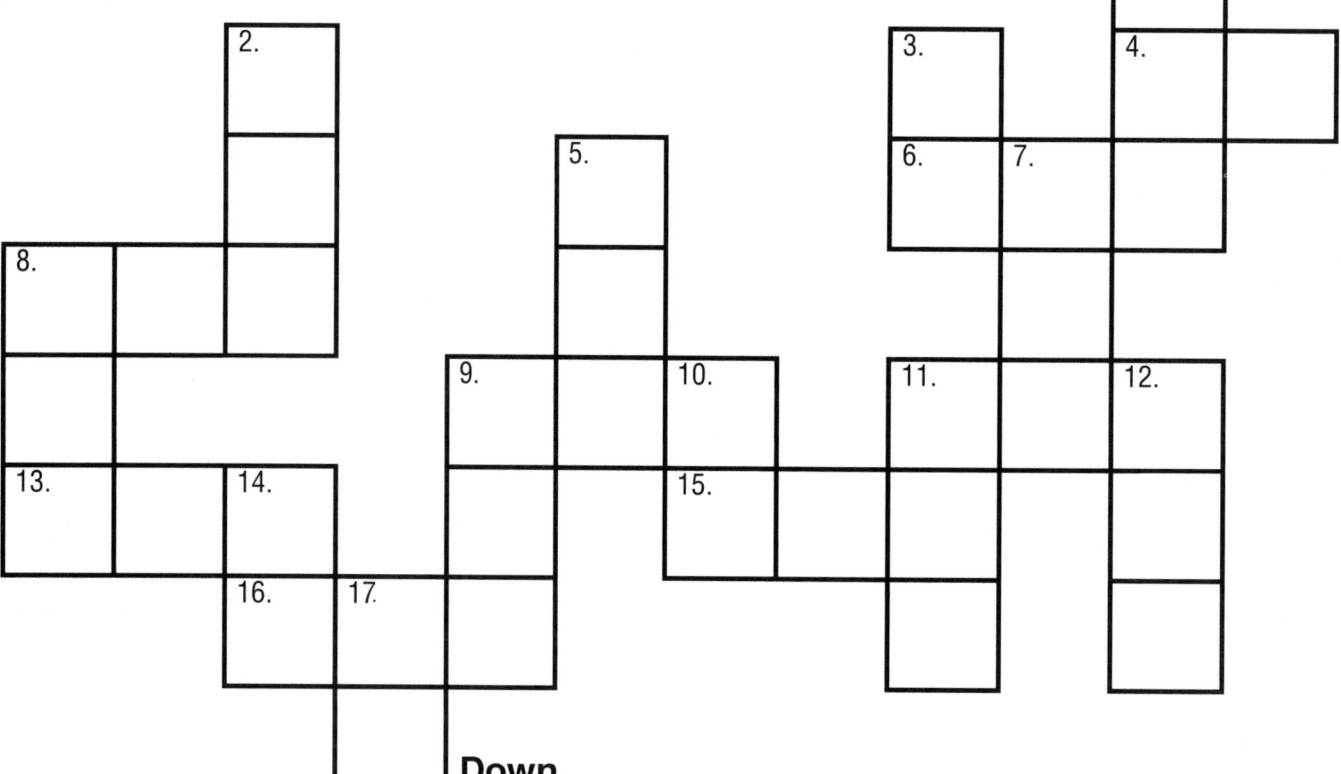

Down

1. 86 x 9 = _____
2. 28 x 7 = _____
3. 31 x 1 = _____
5. 24 x 9 = _____
7. 64 x 5 = _____
8. 38 x 3 = _____
9. 46 x 8 = _____
10. 53 x 1 = _____
11. 85 x 8 = _____
12. 74 x 3 = _____
14. 15 x 3 = _____
17. 89 x 1 = _____

#3908 Practice Makes Perfect: Number Puzzles © Teacher Created Resources, Inc.

Puzzle 18

Multiplication Fun

Solve each multiplication problem. Write each product in the number puzzle.

Across
1. 327 x 3 = _____
3. 335 x 5 = _____
4. 761 x 9 = _____
6. 249 x 2 = _____
9. 861 x 9 = _____
11. 702 x 8 = _____
13. 923 x 8 = _____
14. 678 x 9 = _____
16. 101 x 5 = _____
17. 783 x 3 = _____
18. 785 x 5 = _____

Down
2. 653 x 3 = _____
3. 246 x 8 = _____
5. 474 x 2 = _____
7. 174 x 5 = _____
8. 432 x 8 = _____
10. 326 x 5 = _____
12. 805 x 3 = _____
15. 375 x 7 = _____
16. 149 x 4 = _____

Missing Factors

Puzzle 19

Name That Factor!

Write the missing factor for each multiplication problem on the blank lines below. Then, write the missing factor as a **number word** in the number puzzle. See #2 Across. It has been done for you.

Across

2. 2 x __2__ = 4
4. 2 x _____ = 14
6. 7 x _____ = 35
7. 4 x _____ = 24
8. 7 x _____ = 70
9. 8 x _____ = 64
12. 10 x _____ = 90
14. 5 x _____ = 20
15. 9 x _____ = 27

Down

1. 10 x _____ = 10
3. 9 x _____ = 9
4. 4 x _____ = 24
5. 9 x _____ = 81
6. 3 x _____ = 15
7. 5 x _____ = 35
8. 8 x _____ = 16
10. 1 x _____ = 10
11. 5 x _____ = 15
13. 6 x _____ = 48
14. 2 x _____ = 8

#3908 Practice Makes Perfect: Number Puzzles
© Teacher Created Resources, Inc.

One-Digit Divisors/Two-Digit Dividends/No Remainders

Puzzle 20

Easy to Divide

Solve each division problem. Write each quotient as a **number word** in the number puzzle. See #3 Across. It has been done for you.

Across

3. 14 ÷ 2 = __7__

5. 49 ÷ 7 = _____

8. 48 ÷ 6 = _____

9. 75 ÷ 5 = _____

11. 10 ÷ 10 = _____

12. 36 ÷ 9 = _____

14. 96 ÷ 8 = _____

16. 39 ÷ 3 = _____

18. 16 ÷ 4 = _____

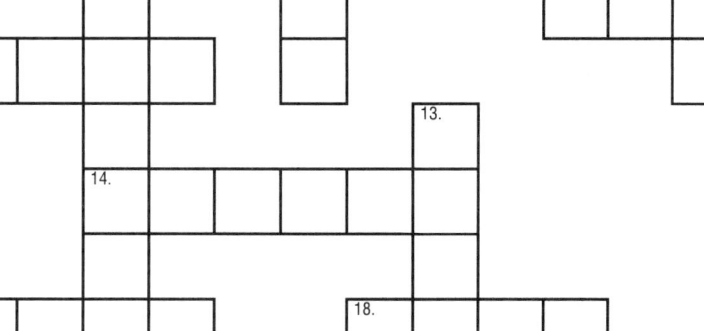

Down

1. 78 ÷ 6 = _____
2. 35 ÷ 7 = _____
4. 22 ÷ 2 = _____
6. 81 ÷ 9 = _____
7. 27 ÷ 9 = _____
9. 56 ÷ 4 = _____

10. 30 ÷ 3 = _____
13. 0 ÷ 15 = _____
15. 18 ÷ 3 = _____
16. 14 ÷ 7 = _____
17. 50 ÷ 5 = _____

Mixed Practice Division

Puzzle 21

More Division Practice

Solve each division problem. Write each quotient in the number puzzle.

Across

2. 51 ÷ 1 = _____

4. 420 ÷ 10 = _____

6. 518 ÷ 7 = _____

8. 384 ÷ 2 = _____

10. 548 ÷ 4 = _____

11. 48 ÷ 3 = _____

12. 695 ÷ 5 = _____

13. 68 ÷ 2 = _____

Down

1. 75 ÷ 5 = _____

3. 84 ÷ 6 = _____

5. 243 ÷ 9 = _____

7. 449 ÷ 1 = _____

8. 68 ÷ 4 = _____

9. 828 ÷ 3 = _____

10. 928 ÷ 8 = _____

11. 918 ÷ 6 = _____

12. 98 ÷ 7 = _____

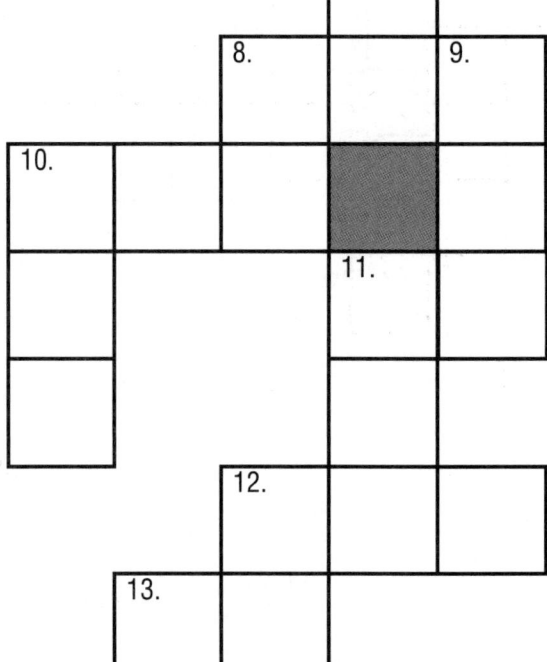

Mixed Practice Multiplication and Division

Puzzle 22

Mixed Practice: Multiplication and Division

Solve each problem and complete the number puzzle.

Across
1. 3,608 ÷ 2 = _____
3. 52,160 ÷ 10 = _____
6. 485 x 8 = _____
8. 4,555 x 5 = _____
10. 784 ÷ 8 = _____
11. 4,013 x 2 = _____
12. 196 x 6 = _____
14. 1,792 x 2 = _____
17. 10,096 ÷ 4 = _____

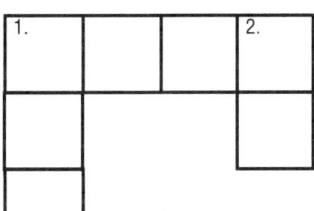
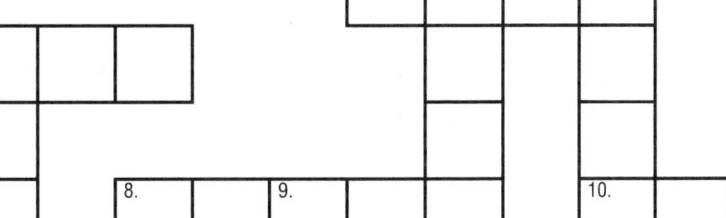
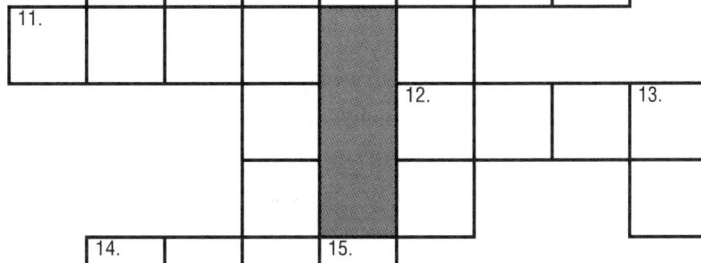
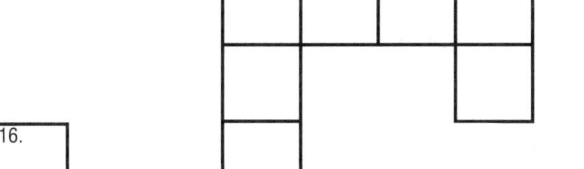

Down
1. 7,725 ÷ 5 = _____
2. 387 ÷ 9 = _____
4. 295 x 9 = _____
5. 6,809 ÷ 1 = _____
7. 812 x 10 = _____
8. 6,717 x 4 = _____
9. 2,438 x 3 = _____
13. 183 ÷ 3 = _____
14. 562 x 7 = _____
15. 264 ÷ 6 = _____
16. 434 ÷ 7 = _____

Decimals in Standard Form

Puzzle 23

Deciphering Decimals

Write each decimal in standard form and complete the number puzzle. Be sure to include the decimal points in the puzzle. See #2 Across. It has been done for you. (Note: Each answer has three digits.)

Across

2. One and fifty-nine hundredths ___1.59___
4. Sixty-five and one tenth _____
6. Seventy-eight and three tenths _____
8. Two and twenty-three hundredths _____
10. Six and eighty-two hundredths _____
12. Nine and forty-two hundredths _____
13. Three and eight hundredths _____
15. Seven and fifty-six hundredths _____
16. Six and twenty-four hundredths _____

Down

1. Forty-nine and five tenths _____
2. Ten and one tenth _____
3. Nine and seventy-seven hundredths _____
5. Five and ninety-seven hundredths _____
7. Eight and sixty-two hundredths _____
9. Thirty-four and eight tenths _____
11. Twenty-three and four tenths _____
12. Nine and fifty-three hundredths _____
14. Eight and forty-six hundredths _____
15. Seven and thirty-four hundredths _____

Puzzle 24

Adding Decimals

Solve each addition problem. Write each sum in the number puzzle. Be sure to include the decimal points in the puzzle. See #1 Across. It has been done for you.

Across

1. .44 + .37 = __.81__
2. .32 + .62 = _____
3. .92 + .53 = _____
4. .73 + .84 = _____
5. .81 + .80 = _____
7. .97 + .19 = _____
8. .80 + .89 = _____
10. .96 + .48 = _____
12. .25 + .28 = _____
13. .43 + .14 = _____

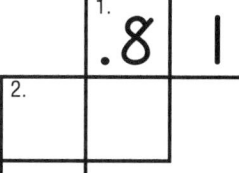
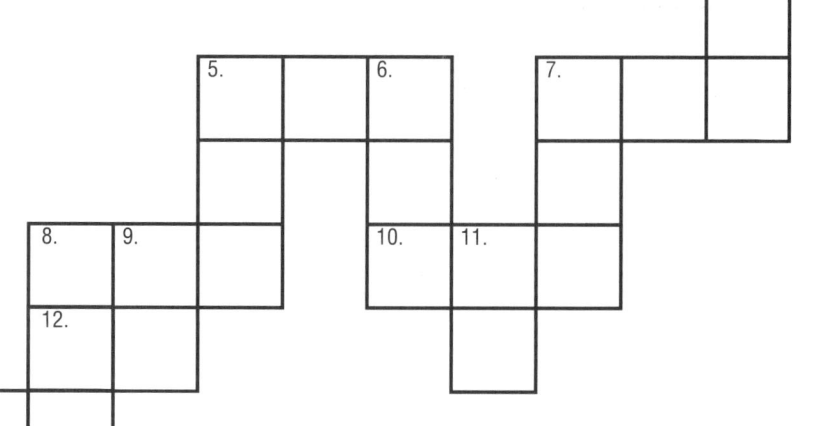

Down

1. .56 + .28 = _____
2. .50 + .45 = _____
3. .65 + .62 = _____
4. .76 + .70 = _____
5. .62 + .77 = _____
6. .17 + .84 = _____
7. .21 + .93 = _____
8. .94 + .63 = _____
9. .51 + .12 = _____
11. .05 + .39 = _____

Subtracting Decimals

Puzzle 25

Subtracting Decimals

Solve each subtraction problem. Write each difference in the number puzzle. Be sure to include the decimal points in the puzzle. See #1 Across. It has been done for you.

Across

1. 9.18 – .92 = __8.26__
3. .47 – .36 = _____
4. .38 – .35 = _____
5. 5.15 – .73 = _____
7. .69 – .38 = _____
8. 9.36 – .12 = _____
10. 8.62 – .01 = _____
12. .85 – .80 = _____
13. 2.82 – .99 = _____

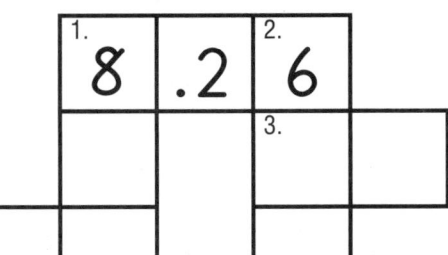

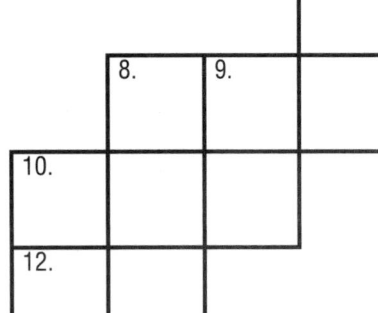

Down

1. 9.07 – .84 = _____
2. 6.64 – .46 = _____
4. .75 – .73 = _____
5. 4.99 – .65 = _____
6. .84 – .43 = _____
8. 9.67 – .02 = _____
9. .31 – .10 = _____
10. 8.08 – .05 = _____
11. .90 – .19 = _____
14. .87 – .06 = _____

#3908 Practice Makes Perfect: Number Puzzles · © Teacher Created Resources, Inc.

Puzzle 26

Adding and Subtracting Decimals

Solve each problem and complete the number puzzle. Be sure to include the decimal points in the puzzle. See #1 Across. It has been done for you.

Across

1. 1.67 + 8.79 = __10.46__
3. 6.44 − 2.14 = _____
4. 2.89 + 3.86 = _____
5. 1.71 + 3.37 = _____
6. 1.93 + 8.62 = _____
8. 2.35 + 5.68 = _____
9. 5.99 − 3.42 = _____
10. 9.37 − 5.86 = _____
12. 5.49 − 5.40 = _____
13. 2.86 + 5.81 = _____
14. 1.79 + 7.71 = _____

Down

1. 4.16 + 8.72 = _____
2. 7.84 − 1.48 = _____
3. 9.59 − 5.24 = _____
5. 8.71 − 3.71 = _____
6. 3.92 + 9.25 = _____
7. 7.84 − 2.44 = _____
9. 7.69 − 5.06 = _____
11. 7.11 − 6.04 = _____
13. 2.46 + 5.93 = _____

Money in Standard Form

Puzzle 27

Money, Money, Money

Write each amount in standard form and complete the number puzzle. Be sure to include the dollar signs and the decimal points in the puzzle. See #2 Across. It has been done for you.

Across

2. Seven dollars and thirty-five cents: __$7.35__
4. Eight dollars and sixty cents: _____
5. Two dollars and fifty-five cents: _____
6. Five dollars and sixty cents: _____
7. One dollar and seventy-five cents: _____
8. One dollar and seventy cents: _____
9. Ten dollars and eighty cents: _____
10. Six dollars and fifteen cents: _____
11. Nine dollars and fifty cents: _____
12. Four dollars and ten cents: _____

Down

1. Four dollars and twenty cents: _____
2. Seven dollars and fifty-five cents: _____
3. Five dollars and twenty-five cents: _____
4. Eight dollars and fifty cents: _____
5. Two dollars and seventy-five cents: _____
7. Ten dollars and twenty cents: _____
8. One dollar and fifty cents: _____
9. One dollar and forty-five cents: _____
10. Six dollars and ninety cents: _____
11. Nine dollars and eighty cents: _____

Puzzle 28

More Money, Money, Money

Write each amount in standard form and complete the number puzzle. Be sure to include the dollar signs and the decimal points in the puzzle. See #3 Across. It has been done for you.

Across

3. Eighty-six dollars and eighty-three cents: $86.83
5. Seventeen dollars and sixty-six cents: _____
7. Ninety-one dollars and forty-nine cents: _____
8. Thirty-one dollars and eighty-four cents: _____
10. Eighty-three dollars and ninety-nine cents: _____
11. Eighty-two dollars and fifteen cents: _____
12. Fifty-four dollars and forty-seven cents: _____
13. Twenty-seven dollars and twenty-eight cents: _____
15. Twenty-three dollars and ninety-six cents: _____
16. Ninety-one dollars and seventy-six cents: _____

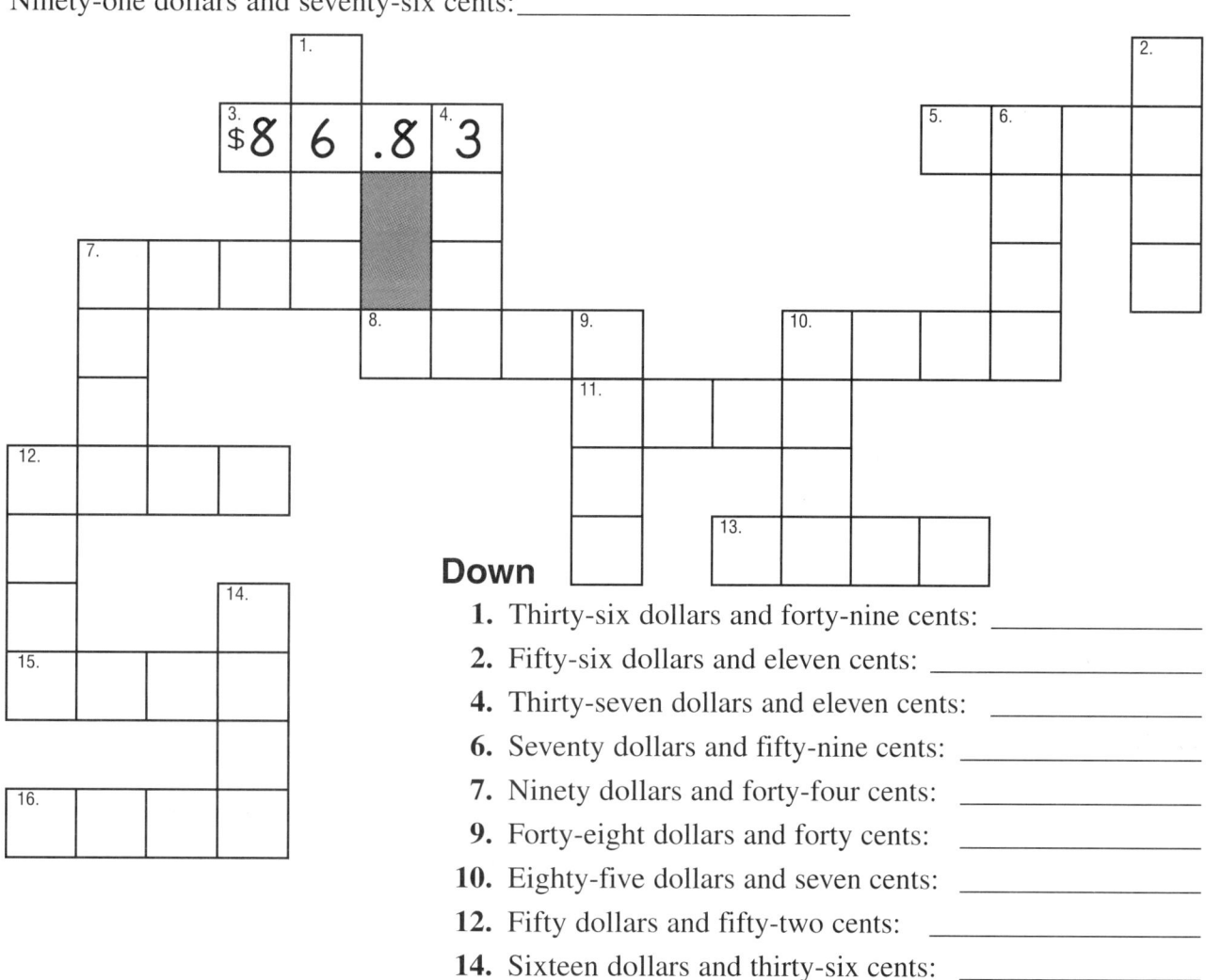

Down

1. Thirty-six dollars and forty-nine cents: _____
2. Fifty-six dollars and eleven cents: _____
4. Thirty-seven dollars and eleven cents: _____
6. Seventy dollars and fifty-nine cents: _____
7. Ninety dollars and forty-four cents: _____
9. Forty-eight dollars and forty cents: _____
10. Eighty-five dollars and seven cents: _____
12. Fifty dollars and fifty-two cents: _____
14. Sixteen dollars and thirty-six cents: _____

Calculating Time in Minutes

Puzzle 29

Does Anybody Have the Time?

Calculate the number of minutes in each amount of time given. Write each answer in the number puzzle.

Across
1. Number of minutes in ten hours: _____
3. Number of minutes at five until the hour: _____
6. Number of minutes in six hours: _____
8. Number of minutes in eight hours: _____
9. Number of minutes in one-half of an hour: _____
10. Number of minutes in half a day: _____
12. Number of minutes in two and one-half hours: _____
13. Number of minutes in three-quarters of an hour: _____
14. Number of minutes in one and one-half hours: _____
15. Number of minutes in one day: _____

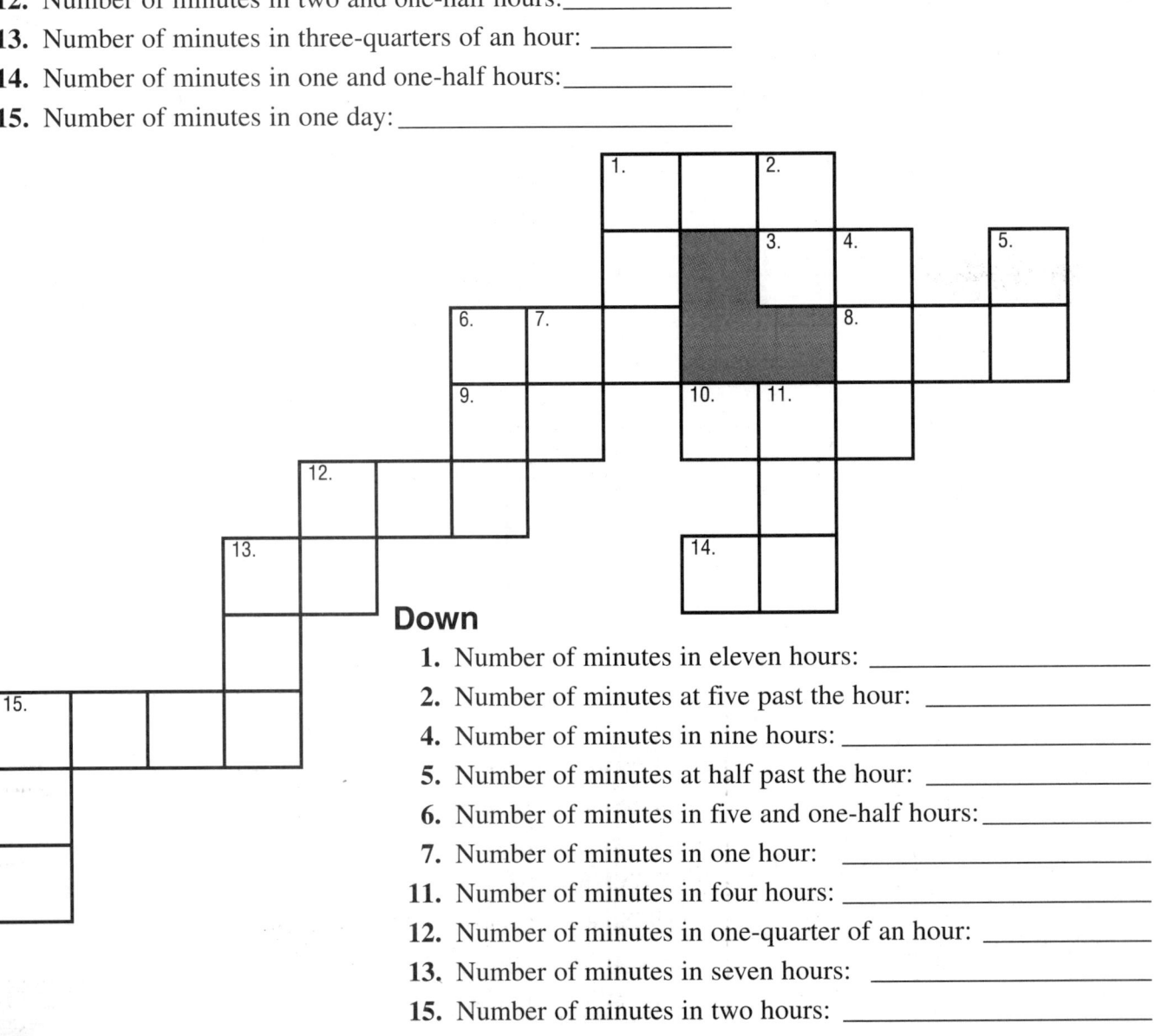

Down
1. Number of minutes in eleven hours: _____
2. Number of minutes at five past the hour: _____
4. Number of minutes in nine hours: _____
5. Number of minutes at half past the hour: _____
6. Number of minutes in five and one-half hours: _____
7. Number of minutes in one hour: _____
11. Number of minutes in four hours: _____
12. Number of minutes in one-quarter of an hour: _____
13. Number of minutes in seven hours: _____
15. Number of minutes in two hours: _____

Writing Time with Minutes

Puzzle 30

Minute by Minute

Write the time shown in each clock in digital format on the lines provided. Then, write the digital times in number puzzle on page 34. You do not need to include the colons in the puzzle. See #1 Across. It has been done for you.

Across

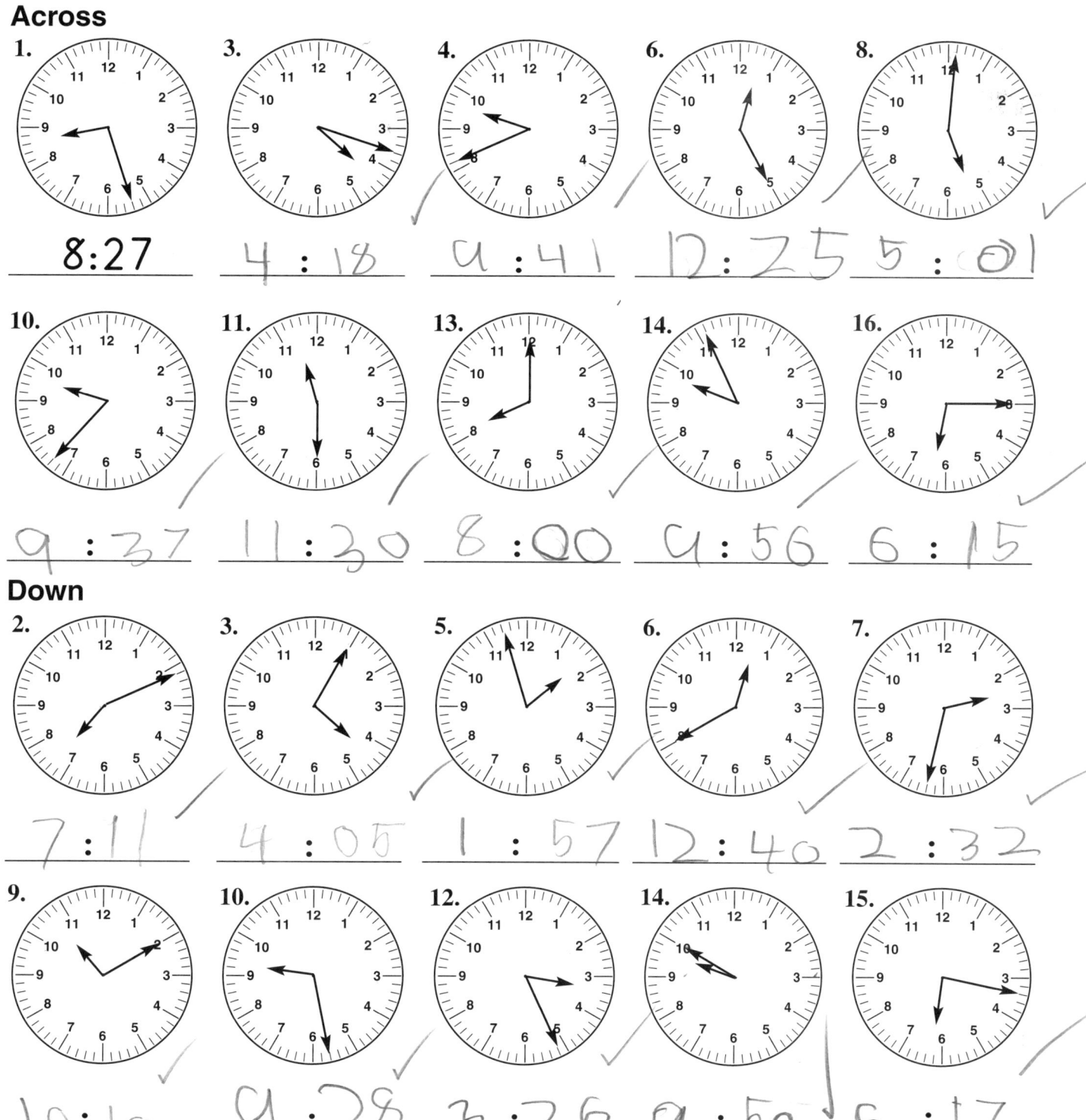

1. 8:27
3. 4:18
4. 9:41
6. 12:25
8. 5:01
10. 9:37
11. 11:30
13. 8:00
14. 9:56
16. 6:15

Down

2. 7:11
3. 4:05
5. 1:57
6. 12:40
7. 2:32
9. 10:10
10. 9:28
12. 3:26
14. 9:50
15. 6:17

© Teacher Created Resources, Inc.   #3908 Practice Makes Perfect: Number Puzzles

Writing Time with Minutes

Puzzle 30

Minute by Minute (cont.)

See page 33 for the Across and Down clues.

Puzzle 31

Pockets Full of Money

Calculate the amount of money that each person has. Write each money amount in the number puzzle on page 36. Be sure to include the dollar signs and the decimal points in the puzzle. See #1 Across. It has been done for you.

Across

1. Steve has seven pennies, three nickels, two dimes, and six quarters. _____ $1.92 _____
2. David has four pennies, six dimes, and four quarters. _____
4. Jack has ten pennies, five dimes, and five quarters. _____
5. Ophelia has eight nickels, nine dimes, and four quarters. _____
6. Reba has nine pennies, two nickels, and six quarters. _____
7. Larry has eight pennies, nine nickels, five dimes, and four quarters. _____
8. Michelle has five pennies, seven nickels, five dimes, and nine quarters. _____
9. Isabel has two pennies, four dimes, and eight quarters. _____
11. Nick has six pennies, three nickels, seven dimes, and two quarters. _____
12. Vince has a penny, three nickels, a dime, and six quarters. _____

Down

1. Taylor has four pennies, five nickels, one dime, and five quarters. _____
2. Frank has five pennies, eight nickels, a dime, and four quarters. _____
3. Kendra has three nickels, three dimes, and three quarters. _____
4. Georgia has nine pennies, two nickels, and ten dimes. _____
5. Ben has eight pennies, eight nickels, three dimes, and seven quarters. _____
6. Cassie has five pennies, two nickels, six dimes, and four quarters. _____
7. Eddie has seven pennies, four nickels, eight dimes, and seven quarters. _____
8. Paul has a penny, nine nickels, nine dimes, and nine quarters. _____
10. Ashley has six pennies, a nickel, three dimes, and ten quarters. _____
11. Henry has a penny, three nickels, a dime, and four quarters. _____

Counting Money

Puzzle 31

Pockets Full of Money (cont.)

See page 35 for the Across and Down clues.

Puzzle 32

At the Game Shop

Solve each word problem. Write each answer as a **number word** in the number puzzle on page 38. See #1 Across. It has been done for you.

Across

1. There are 75 game tokens in five bags. How many game tokens are in each bag? __15__

3. There are 54 coins in nine boxes. How many coins are in each box? _____

4. Exactly 84 houses are sold in six sets. How many houses are in each set? _____

7. There are 44 cars sold in four containers. How many cars are in each container? _____

9. Altogether, 28 playing boards are on two shelves. How many playing boards are on each shelf? _____

11. A total of 90 blocks are in ten sets. How many blocks are in each set? _____

13. There are 48 beads in four packets. How many beads are in each packet? _____

15. A total of 60 pens are sold in five sets. How many pens are in each set? _____

16. Exactly 80 decks of playing cards are shown in spinner racks. Each spinner rack holds ten decks of cards. How many spinner racks are there? _____

17. Exactly 15 dominoes are sold in three sets. How many dominoes are there in each set? _____

Down

2. Altogether, 65 checkers are divided into five plastic cylinders. How many checkers are in each cylinder? _____

4. Exactly 36 plastic monkeys are sold in nine sets. How many plastic monkeys are in each set? _____

5. A total of 90 sets of funny money are sold with ten sets to a pack. How many packs of funny money are there? _____

6. A total of 21 plastic cherries are divided into three bags. How many plastic cherries are there in each bag? _____

8. A total of 24 calling cards are sold in three packs. How many calling cards are in each pack? _____

9. Exactly 45 shoelaces are divided into three small shoe boxes. How many shoelaces are in each box? _____

10. A total of 25 wooden pegs are sold in five separate miniature barrels. How many pegs are in each barrel? _____

12. Altogether, 20 batteries are sold in packs of two. How many packs of batteries are there? _____

14. A store sells 60 marbles in six complete marble sets. How many marbles are in each set? _____

15. Exactly 18 extra spinners are sold six to an envelope. How many envelopes of spinners are there? _____

Word Problems with Division

Puzzle 32

At the Game Shop (cont.)

See page 37 for the Across and Down clues.

Puzzle 33

Party Supplies

Use the chart below to find the difference or total number of party supplies sold in each word problem. Write each answer directly onto the number puzzle on page 40.

Sales of Party Supplies

Item	Quantity	Item	Quantity
Balloons	1,053	Noise Makers	8,982
Candles	1,614	Party Hats	1,026
Confetti Packs	5,743	Piñatas	6,586
Costumes	7,846	Streamers	4,767
Masks	4,732	Whistles	4,937

Across

1. Abra found the difference between the number of whistles and candles sold.
3. Jerome found the difference between the number of confetti packs and party hats sold.
5. Tyler counted the total number of costumes and candles sold.
6. Eugene counted the total number of noise makers and whistles sold.
7. Helen counted the total number of candles and piñatas sold.
10. Ivan counted the total number of confetti packs and streamers sold.
12. Paul found the difference between the number of piñatas and confetti packs sold.
14. Bea counted the total number of balloons and costumes sold.
16. Kurt found the difference between the number of costumes and piñatas sold.
17. Janell found the difference between the number of masks and party hats sold.

Down

1. Mark found the difference between the number of masks and balloons sold.
2. Lindsey found the difference between the number of costumes and whistles sold.
4. Lee found the total number of piñatas and balloons sold.
6. Trevor found the total number of masks and confetti packs sold.
8. Shane found the difference between the number of streamers and candles sold.
9. Charlotte counted the total number of party hats and noise makers sold.
11. Tom found the difference between the number of noise makers and balloons sold.
13. Stevie found the difference between the number of noise makers and streamers sold.
15. Willy found the total number of whistles and masks sold.

Puzzle 33

Party Supplies (cont.)

See page 39 for the Across and Down clues.

Puzzle 34

Arts and Crafts Store

Use the chart below to calculate the amount of money each person spent at the arts and crafts store. Write each money amount in the number puzzle on page 42. Be sure to include the dollar signs and the decimal points in the puzzle. See #1 Across. It has been done for you.

Clay (all colors)	$3.11 a pound	Markers	$5.75 a box
Construction Paper	$6.62 a pack	Paint (all colors)	$0.84 a bottle
Crayons	$1.70 a box	Project Kits	$10.89 each
Glue	$1.02 a bottle	Scissors	$1.79 each
Glue Gun	$8.13 each	Yarn (all colors)	$2.90 a skein

Across

1. Frisco bought two boxes of markers. $11.50
3. Milla bought three bottles of glue.
4. Sean bought five boxes of markers and four boxes of crayons.
5. Billy bought six project kits.
7. Rebecca bought a glue gun and five bottles of paint.
9. Will bought nine bottles of glue.
10. Abby bought four skeins of brown yarn, two skeins of white yarn, and two skeins of gray yarn.
12. Tabitha bought nine bottles of glue and four pounds of clay.
16. Olivia bought eight boxes of crayons.
17. Parker bought three skeins of yarn and two boxes of markers.

Down

2. Dean bought three packs of construction paper.
3. Vincent bought two packs of construction paper and two project kits.
4. Neville bought one bottle of white paint and one skein of pink yarn.
6. Horace bought two bottles of yellow paint, two bottles of green paint, two bottles of purple paint, and one bottle of black paint.
8. Louis bought five packs of construction paper.
11. Katie bought four glue guns.
13. Karen bought two skeins of red yarn, one skein of green yarn, and two skeins of blue yarn.
14. Ivana bought three pounds of purple clay, three pounds of red clay, and three pounds of blue clay.
15. Edwina bought seven pairs of scissors.
16. Gayle bought six boxes of crayons.

Puzzle 34

Arts and Crafts Store (cont.)

See page 41 for the Across and Down clues.

Answer Key

Puzzle 1 Page 4
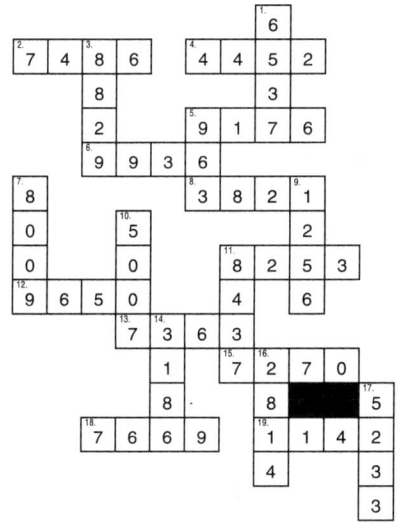

Puzzle 4 Page 7

Puzzle 2 Page 5

Puzzle 5 Page 8
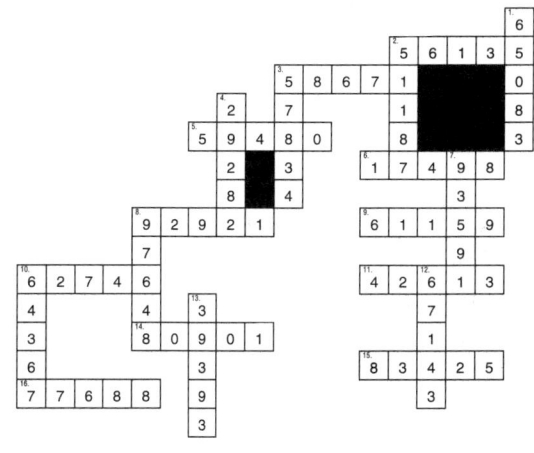

Puzzle 3 Page 6

Puzzle 6 Page 9

Answer Key

Puzzle 7 Page 10

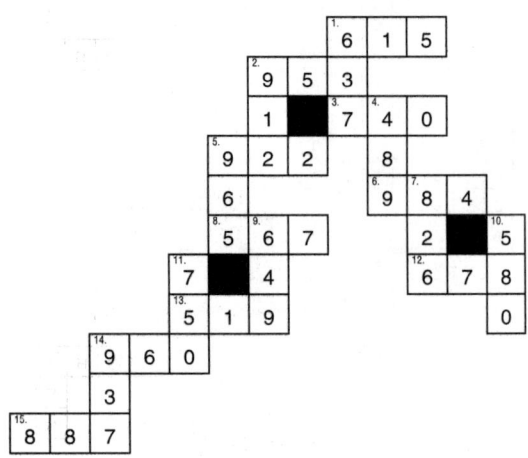

Puzzle 10 Page 13

Puzzle 8 Page 11

Puzzle 11 Page 14

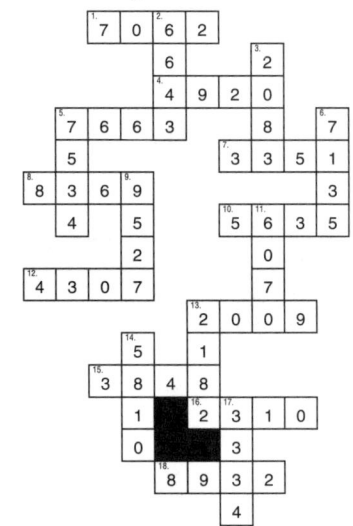

Puzzle 9 Page 12

Puzzle 12 Page 15

#3908 Practice Makes Perfect: Number Puzzles — © Teacher Created Resources, Inc.

Answer Key

Puzzle 13 Page 16

Puzzle 14 Page 17

Puzzle 15 Page 18

Puzzle 16 Page 19

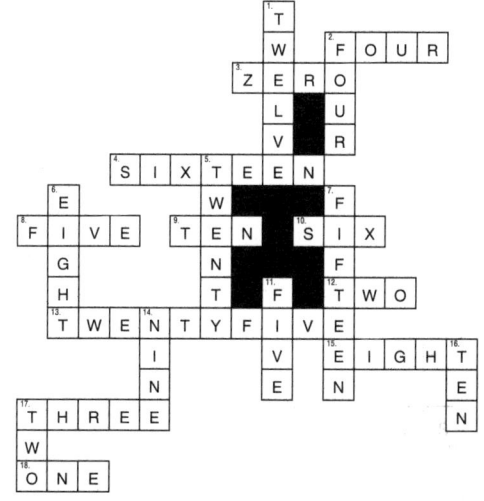

Puzzle 17 Page 20

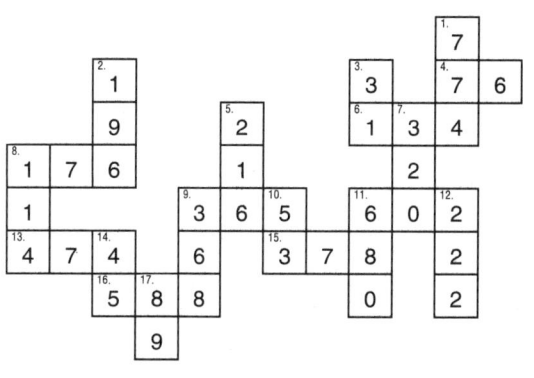

Puzzle 18 Page 21

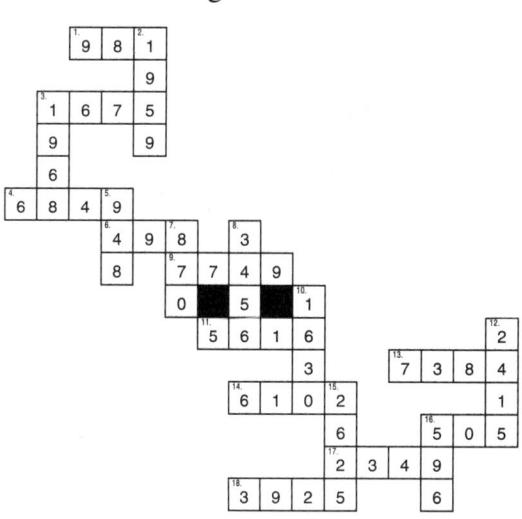

Answer Key

Puzzle 19 Page 22

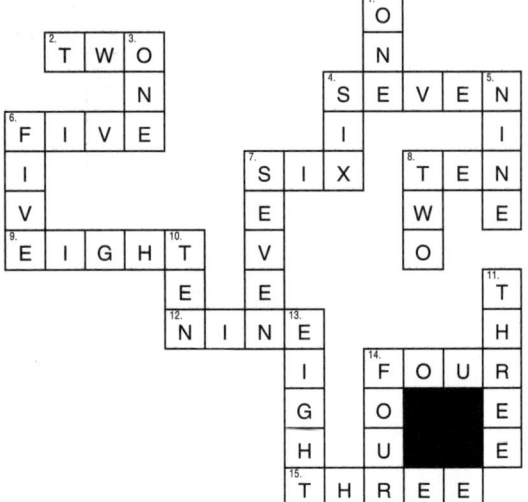

Puzzle 20 Page 23

Puzzle 21 Page 24

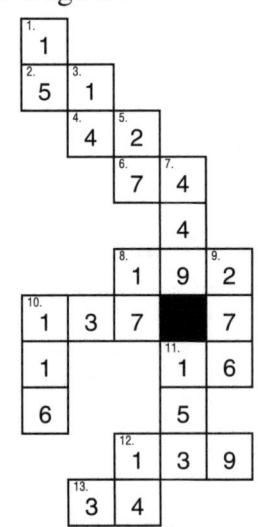

Puzzle 22 Page 25

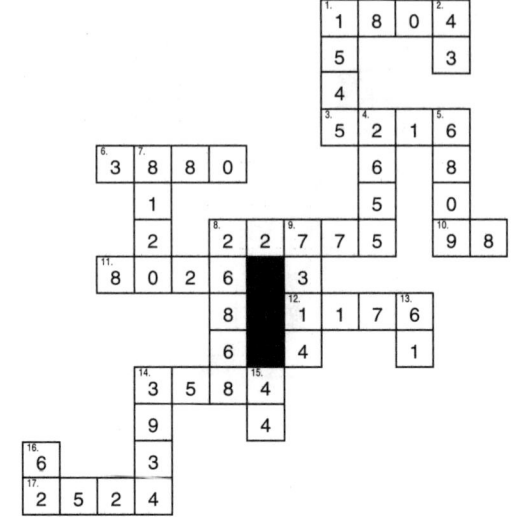

Puzzle 23 Page 26

Puzzle 24 Page 27

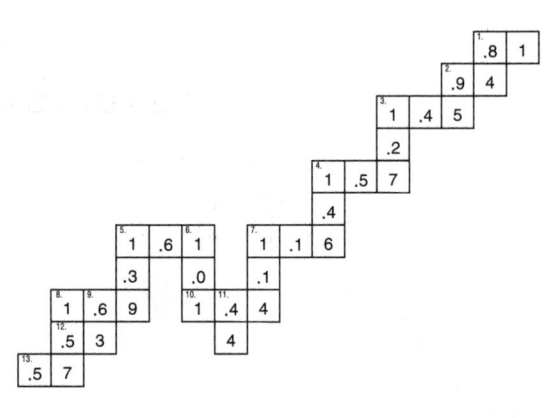

Answer Key

Puzzle 25 Page 28

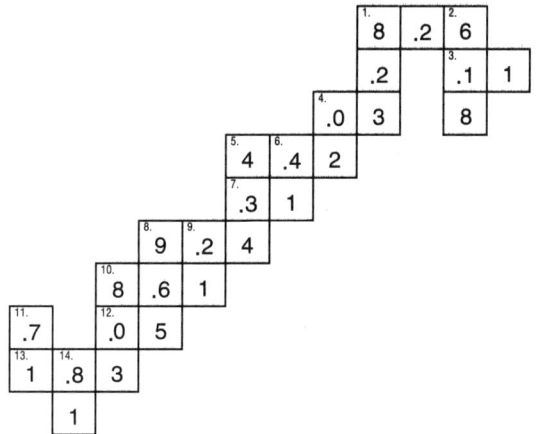

Puzzle 26 Page 29

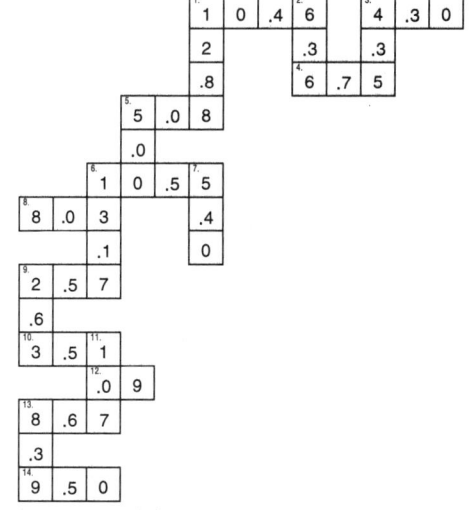

Puzzle 27 Page 30

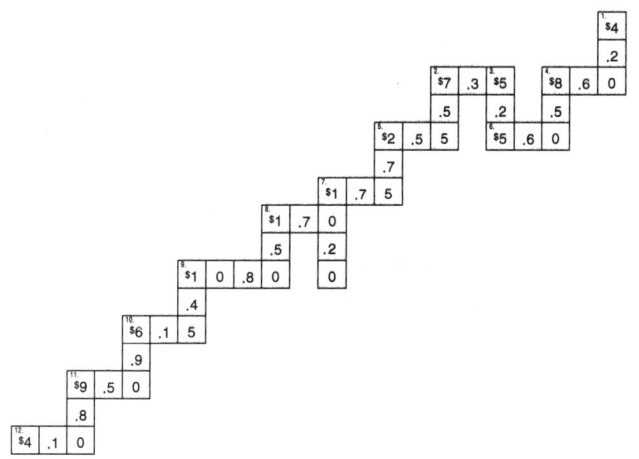

Puzzle 28 Page 31

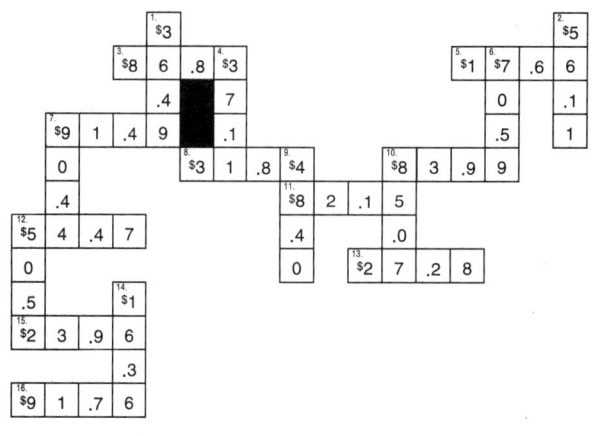

Puzzle 29 Page 32

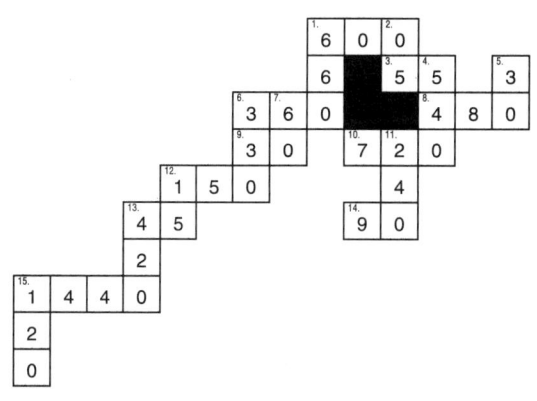

Puzzle 30 Page 34

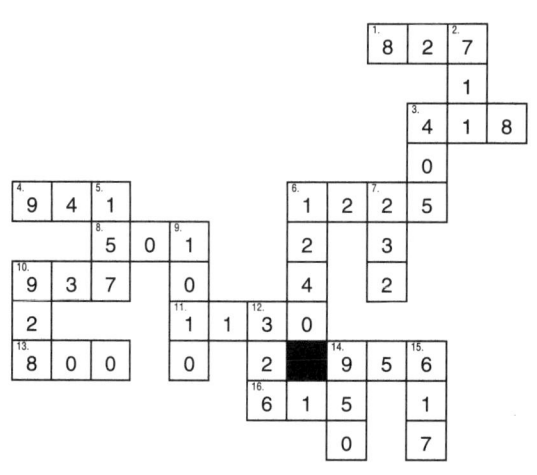

Answer Key

Puzzle 31   Page 36

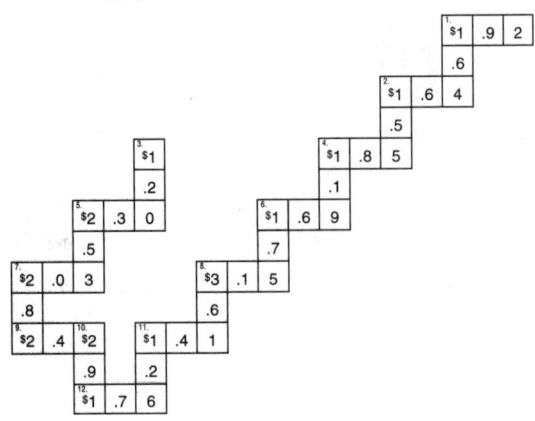

Puzzle 34   Page 42

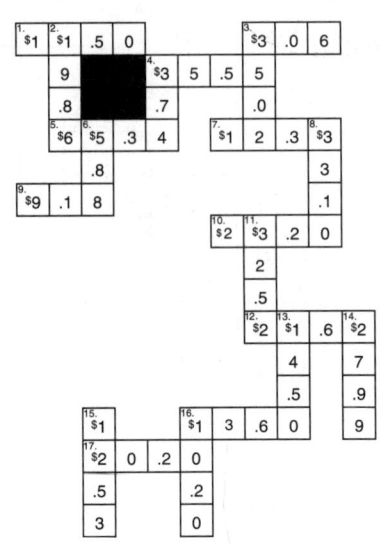

Puzzle 32   Page 38

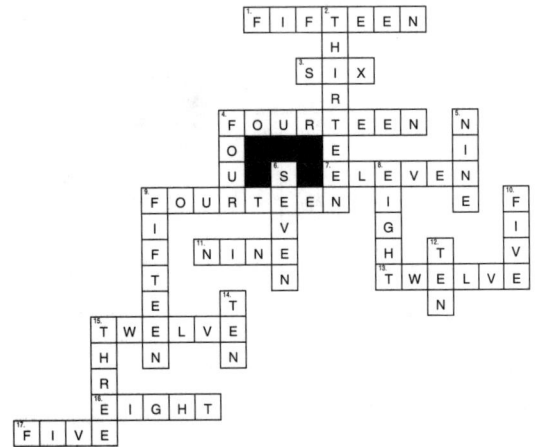

Puzzle 33   Page 40

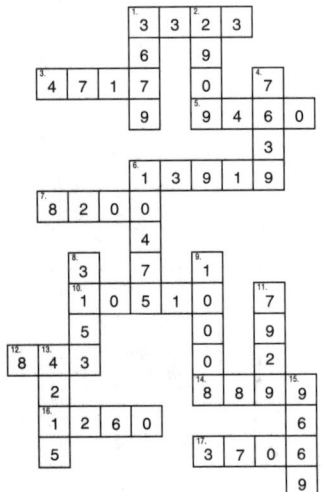